THE
FUNNIEST
FOREST
QUOTES...
EVER!

Also available

THE FUNNIEST FOREST QUOTES... EVER!

by Gordon Law

Printed in Europe and the USA
ISBN: 9798692993823
Imprint: Independently published

Photos courtesy of: Influential Photography/Shutterstock.com; Photo Works/Shutterstock.com.

Contents

Introduction

"I wouldn't say I was the best manager in the business. But I was in the top one," reflected Brian Clough in typically modest fashion.

The charismatic boss is one of the greatest ever after leading Nottingham Forest to a league title, before securing back-to-back European Cups.

Clough's caustic wit also made him one of the funniest personalities in the game. Whether it was firing broadsides at his players, rival managers or chairmen, nobody was safe.

The king of one-liners, Clough claimed Kenny Burns was the "ugliest player I ever signed", bemoaned that "acne is a bigger problem than injuries" for his young team and he once compared football to childbirth.

Former midfielder Martin O'Neill, who often found himself in Clough's firing line, has followed his lead in providing entertaining sound bites since moving into the dugout.

Dave Bassett came out with comical quips, there's been bonkers remarks from Frank Clark and daft statements from Billy Davies.

Forest players too have made us laugh, from Larry Lloyd's humorous observations to zingers from Mark Crossley and John Robertson's off-the-field anecdotes.

Many of their foot-in-mouth moments and more can be found in this unique collection of funny Forest quotes and I hope you laugh as much reading this book as I did in compiling it.

Gordon Law

THE FUNNIEST FOREST QUOTES... EVER!

MANAGING JUST FINE

"I'm fed up with him pointing to his grey hair and saying the England job has aged him 10 years. If he doesn't like it, why doesn't he go back to his orchard in Suffolk."

Brian Clough on England manager Bobby Robson

"We are a young side that will only get younger."

Paul Hart

"If it meant getting three points on Saturday, I would shoot my grandmother. Not nastily. I would just hurt her."

Brian Clough during a bad run of form

"Doing well in football is like childbirth – it doesn't happen overnight."

Brian Clough

"I could have signed [Dennis] Bergkamp. His agent rang us but I wasn't interested. Bryan [Roy] is more dangerous, he's got more pace... He's the best foreigner in Britain."

Frank Clark

"One of the few players as nasty off the field as on it."

Brian Clough is not a big fan of Archie Gemmill

"We would never drink the tea at Anfield. You don't know what the cheating b*stards have put in it."

Brian Clough on playing Liverpool in the 1970s

"I think they sent the forms by pigeon and it obviously flew past us."

Dave Bassett after the paperwork for Brian O'Neil's loan deal from Celtic didn't arrive in time for him to play against Liverpool

"I've got a young team. Acne is a bigger problem than injuries."

Brian Clough

"If God had meant football to be played in the air, he'd have put grass in the sky."

Brian Clough

"You'd think we'd won the European Cup that night – we were drunk on success. Which, bearing in mind it was the Anglo-Scottish Cup, was like being drunk on half a pint of shandy."

Brian Clough on winning the trophy in 1977

"We pass each other on the A52 going to work on most days of the week. But if his car broke down and I saw him thumbing a lift, I wouldn't pick him up. I'd run him over."

Brian Clough on Derby boss Peter Taylor

"I had to go. Towards the end I felt like a turkey waiting for Christmas."

Frank Clark after leaving as manager

"I'm as bad a judge of strikers as Walter Winterbottom – he gave me only two caps."

Brian Clough on the ex-England manager

"Floats like a butterfly and stings like one, too."

Brian Clough on Trevor Brooking

"The only bad thing about our situation is the situation itself."

Gary Megson

"The only person certain of boarding the bus to Wembley for the Littlewoods Cup Final is Albert Kershaw, and he'll be driving it."
Brian Clough keeps his players grounded

"If that happens, I'll get an MBE, an OBE and a visit to see the Pope!"
Billy Davies will be chuffed if Forest win promotion

"There are bigger heads than mine in this division – Howard Wilkinson springs to mind."
Brian Clough, who later apologised for the remark

"I hope you were as delighted as I was last week when Nelson Mandela was freed from a South African jail. But what I hadn't bargained for was that his release was going to cut across the start of our Littlewoods Cup Final."
Brian Clough

"Come Saturday, it's all about starting with a blank sheet of football."
Billy Davies

"He is like a lot of people who know a job. They think they know a little bit more than they do."
Brian Clough on Malcolm Allison

"Away games are more like school outings."

Brian Clough on his young Forest side leading the First Division in 1986

"Me and the missus sat down last night, put the players' names in a hat and drew them out."

Stuart Pearce after winning his first game as acting manager

"I asked my coach driver to try to knock [Paul] Gascoigne down if he sees him at Wembley. I don't think we'll stop him otherwise."

Brian Clough ahead of the 1991 FA Cup Final

"The wraps are off England's new kit – and I'm saying now I don't like it. It has the look of one of my mother's old pinnies!"

Brian Clough on the 1980 Admiral strip

"We will accept Deutschmarks, francs, lira, pesetas, guilders or Scottish pounds. Any currency will do, just to get the bloke off our hands."

Dave Bassett on Pierre van Hooijdonk

"Jim Leighton is a rare bird – a Scottish goalkeeper that can be relied on."

Brian Clough

"It was like buying a Van Gogh and sticking it away in a bank vault."

Brian Clough on Charlie Nicholas being stuck in Arsenal's reserves

"I wrote out my best 11 players and Liz said, 'Where's Crossley?' I'd forgotten the goalkeeper."

Caretaker boss Stuart Pearce

"Can't avoid the truth. Can't make it look better than it is. Only one thing to be said. We're in the sh*t."

Brian Clough on fighting relegation in 1993

"I knew it would be bad at Forest. I just didn't know how awful. Our training ground was about as attractive as Siberia in mid-winter without your coat on, our training kit looked like something you got from the Oxfam shop. We barely had a player in the first team I thought could play... I even had to teach them to dress smartly, take their hands out of their pockets and stop slouching."

Brian Clough on his first campaign at the club

"The only agent back then was 007 – and he sh*gged women, not entire football clubs."

Brian Clough

"I'm telling you, there wouldn't have been more of an outcry if the Welsh FA had dug up Dr Crippen and given him the chance of going to the next World Cup."

Brian Clough on the reaction to being offered the Wales job

"I didn't have to talk money with them. I could buy the bloody Welsh FA... I told them that if they were hard up they needn't hire a coach for matches. I'd use my company car. It's a big Mercedes and I'd get most of their squad in it."

Brian Clough on negotiating terms with the Wales FA

"We treat our European matches like seaside holidays, a break from the factory floor of the Football League. We enjoy ourselves, even though we pack our boots rather than a bucket and spade."
Brian Clough on the 1979 European campaign

"We took one sugar in our tea instead of two, we used margarine rather than butter, and we all drank Tizer instead of Scotch because we got thruppence back on the empty bottle."
Brian Clough on Forest's financial woes

Q: "Why are Forest at the bottom of the table?"
Brian Clough: "We're crap."

"We couldn't have beaten a team from Come Dancing."

Brian Clough on the Forest side that he inherited

"Listen, our lot are so young most of 'em still believe in Father Christmas. I haven't the heart to tell them the truth."

Brian Clough on his youthful squad

"I didn't legislate for the fact that when the FA get into their stride they make the Mafia look like kindergarten material."

Brian Clough on getting an England job interview in 1977

"I'd want them to tell me: Is it the birds, is it the booze or is it the betting? 'Cos most of us are susceptible to one of those things. If I find out that someone likes a bet, I can watch the size of his wallet. If I find out someone likes to chase women, I can see whether his fly is undone. If someone likes a beer, I'll get close enough to smell his breath in the morning. Now that's management."

Brian Clough on what he says to new signings

"I'd love all of us to play football the way Frank Sinatra sings... all that richness in the sound and every word perfect."

Brian Clough on his football philosophy

"When anyone mentions Justin Fashanu to me, I say one thing. I didn't buy him. It had nowt to do with me. The person who did buy him didn't do his job properly."

Brian Clough fires shots at Peter Taylor

"The only thing I've ever seen catch a ball on its nose from 14 feet in the air was a seal I watched as a kid at Blackpool Tower circus."

Brian Clough hates long-ball football

"Bill Nicholson used to say that a pat on the back isn't too far from a kick up the a*se. He was right."

Brian Clough

THE FUNNIEST FOREST QUOTES... EVER!

MEDIA CIRCUS

Journalist: "Do Forest have a chance of staying up?"

Ron Atkinson: "Did you ask the captain of the Titanic the same question?"

"Bloody driver got lost. Hey, I reckon his last job was driving Rommel's staff car."

Brian Clough on why he turned up late for a media conference in Cologne in 1979

TV reporter: "Can I have a word from you, Brian?"

Brian Clough: "Of course. Goodbye."

On his last game as manager

"You'll have to stop writing about the bleedin'
figure and concentrate on the football now. But,
before you do, having picked up five points
from the previous 15 games, that's six points
from four undefeated since I arrived."

New Forest manager Joe Kinnear

"It's getting to him... just look at him next time
he's on TV. He never looks at the interviewer
and comes out with baffling gibberish. The
cameraman deserves a bonus for keeping his
head in the frame."

**Brian Clough on Coventry boss Gordon
Strachan**

THE FUNNIEST FOREST QUOTES... EVER!

Mike Channon: "We've got to get bodies in the box. The French do it, the Italians do it, the Brazilians do it."

Brian Clough: "Even educated bees do it."

The ITV World Cup pundits in 1986

"There are still some things that baffle me about the bloke [Robert Maxwell]. Like why he loves seeing his mug across the back pages, because Robert Redford he ain't."

Brian Clough

Reporter: "Tommy Gaynor not in the squad?"

Brian Clough: "He's Irish. He probably fell over coming back from the pub!"

Billy Davies: "I see on social media that you and I should race on social media for a pork pie."

Reporter Neil Moxley: "Yeah, go on."

The manager issues a challenge

"Nottingham Forest have confirmed today that they will be making no comment on the considerable media speculation surrounding the future of manager Steve McClaren."

A club statement to comment they will not be commenting

"True fame is when the newspapers spell your name right in Karachi."

Brian Clough

THE FUNNIEST FOREST QUOTES... EVER!

PLAYER POWER

"Cloughie called me Edward. I told him I preferred Teddy. He said, 'Right you are, Edward'."

Teddy Sheringham

"He was a rat, a snake, and he still keeps saying things about me. He is the worst I've come across."

Pierre van Hooijdonk on Dave Bassett

"The gaffer thought Liverpool were the sort of club who put things in your tea. He used to tell us, 'Don't drink it. The cheating b*stards probably put something in it'. At Anfield, he wouldn't drink anything that wasn't sealed."

Stuart Pearce on Brian Clough

"We have to keep his feet on the ground. That's my responsibility as a senior player. If he keeps doing what he is doing, the sky is the limit."

Andy Reid loves a metaphor when praising Jamie Paterson

Q: "Who do you room with and what's his most annoying habit?"

A: "Des Lyttle. He suffers from bad wind."

Jason Lee

"I've seen big men hide in corridors to avoid him. He can make you feel desperate for his approval."

Martin O'Neill on Brian Clough

"He used to join in training and he couldn't move. We were a Premier League team with a 60-year-old running down the wing."

Alan Rodgers on Ron Atkinson

"When I started earning a living 15 years ago, I was told I would never be as good as Brian Clough, never score as many goals, or do this or that like Brian Clough – and most of the time it was him telling me."

Nigel Clough on life as Brian's son

"I couldn't give a sh*t what Pierre [van Hooijdonk] does next."

Steve Stone doesn't hold back

"I went in [to see Brian Clough] shaking with fear to ask for a pay rise. I accepted a whisky and a wage cut."

Martin O'Neill

"As a coach he was inexperienced and unsuccessful, leaving the entire organisation and training work to his assistants because he wanted to play himself."

Bryan Roy doesn't rate Stuart Pearce

Q: "What did you think of Clough calling you a scruffy git?"

John Robertson: "What about the time he said I was like Picasso? I knew Cloughie loved me."

"A hooligan from Birmingham City called Kenny Burns and a little midfield nasty-man called Archie Gemmill."

Larry Lloyd on his teammates

"I used to fall asleep under Dougie's team when I was watching in the stands."

Ex-caretaker manager Ian McParland on Dougie Freedman

"He came with this briefcase every day so I broke into it once. We thought it would hold the secrets of a football world but there was just a hairdryer and a gold American Express card."

Alan Rodgers on Ron Atkinson

"We had a difference of opinion. I thought I was brilliant, he didn't."

Martin O'Neill on Brian Clough

"When it comes to Pierre's previous comments and the way his teammates regard him, well, he should remember that elephants never forget."

Dave Beasant on Van Hooijdonk

"The black players at Forest always had the last laugh when we got into the showers. Chris Fairclough was nicknamed 'Mamba'. I'll leave the rest to your imagination."

Jim McInally

"When Forest's England players went off on international duty, Cloughie used to say, 'Don't get injured'. When I went off with Northern Ireland, all he said to me was, 'Don't come back'."

Martin O'Neill

"Regarding myself and Stuart [Pearce], we had a working understanding and that was all!"

Tommy Gaynor

"Cloughie had four nicknames for me. He used to call me 'Sh*thouse', 'Imbecile' and 'Barnsley'. And when I got into the team regularly, he started to call me 'Jigsaw'."

Mark Crossley

"He'd put his fat a*se to the right – and then, hey presto, he was off, down the left... He was slower even than me, but that little fat b*stard was a magician."

Larry Lloyd on John Robertson

"He would two-foot his granny if you asked him to."

Jack Lester on Ryan Yates

"The only reason they asked you on that beer ad is because you are the biggest pub manager in the country."

Pierre van Hooijdonk to Ron Atkinson who had just appeared in a Carling TV advert

CAN YOU MANAGE?

"It's a beautiful city, with lovely people. I'm particularly fond of the River Trent – blow me, I've been walking on it for the past 18 years."
Brian Clough on being named a freeman of Nottingham

"I'm 52 now and I don't want to be turning up at muddy training grounds for the rest of my life."
Dave Bassett on being appointed general manager

"There was talk of a stand being named after me. But there was nothing, not even a toilet. They could have had the Brian Clough Bog."
Brian Clough before he got his wish

"I think on occasions I have been big-headed. But I call myself Big Head to remind myself not to be."

Brian Clough

"I think they may be confusing 'negative' with 'organised', and I'm not making any apologies for that."

New Forest boss Alex McLeish defends his over-cautious style

"If the BBC ran a Crap Decision of the Month competition on Match of the Day, I'd walk it."

Brian Clough as Forest struggle in the league

"It's a pain in the a*se but you have to live with it. You can't break wind without names like [Brian] Clough and [Garry] Birtles being mentioned."

Joe Kinnear on living up to the greats

"I can't promise to give the team talk in Welsh, but from now on I shall be taking my holidays in Porthcawl and I've a complete set of Harry Secombe albums."

Brian Clough on being offered the job of Wales manager in 1988

"Manager of England? Too late. I'm too old."

Brian Clough, aged 44

"I am staying here until they shoot me because I am finishing after that."

Brian Clough in 1987

"I mentioned retiring to the wife and she said, 'Don't even think about it'."

Dave Bassett has to stay out the house

"You never say never because you don't know what's around the corner."

Frank Clark loves a cliche after leaving Forest

"I'm fat, 50 and worn out."

Brian Clough in 1985

Q: "People say you rule by fear?"

Brian Clough: "If that's the case, why are so many players willing to play for me? And why do so many come back to this club after leaving it? Perhaps they liked my singing."

"I'm going nowhere. Resignations are for prime ministers and cabinets and those caught with their trousers down, not for me."

Brian Clough

"It's easy enough to get to Ireland. Just a straight walk across the Irish Sea as far as I'm concerned."

Brian Clough on applying for the Ireland job

"I listened to a phone-in recently and heard people saying, 'Ferguson's lost the plot' or 'Wenger can't do this or that'. It's completely illogical. I don't go where electricians work saying, 'You've wired this wrong', but people are free to say we know nothing about our profession."

Colin Calderwood

"You have to say nice things to people you don't like and nasty things to people you do. If you can manage that, you're on the right lines. All you have to worry about then is results, finding new players, keeping supporters happy, finding Barnet's ground on a wet Wednesday night, keeping the chairman happy and picking the right team."

Caretaker boss Stuart Pearce

"They say Rome wasn't built in a day, but I wasn't on that particular job."

Brian Clough

"When my kids attempt to take the mickey out of me by asking me to produce my O and A levels, I run upstairs, grab my medals and bang them down on the table. And then I tell them, 'They're the O levels in my industry'."

Brian Clough

"Me? Rely on footballers? That's crap. If I relied on footballers, I would have been out of a job 20 years ago."

Brian Clough in 1983

"My wife says 'OBE' stands for Old Big 'Ead."

Brian Clough

"It's going to be my epitaph, isn't it? Deep in the sh*t, where he started."

Dave Bassett's side is struggling

"Like a woman, I might exercise my prerogative to change my mind."

Brian Clough on announcing retirement

"I could manage England part-time – and still walk the dog."

Brian Clough in 1993

THE FUNNIEST FOREST QUOTES... EVER!

BOARDROOM BANTER

"As far as I'm concerned the manager's position remains unchanged. I know nothing about Ron Atkinson."

Chief executive Phil Soar speaking on Monday, giving manager Dave Bassett a vote of confidence

"Nottingham Forest approached me last night and I agreed that I would consider their offer."

Ron Atkinson got offered Bassett's job on the Tuesday

"Football hooligans? Well, there are the 92 club chairmen for a start."

Brian Clough

"I just felt it was a bad decision all round."

Nigel Doughty on appointing Steve McClaren

"On occasions he's been known to dress like a Christmas tree. But he doesn't only sing better than the other 91 chairmen, he also talks more sense than 95 per cent of them."

Brian Clough on Watford chief Elton John

"The thing that worries me about retirement is that I'll have to sit with directors and directors' wives who have no idea about football. To sit among that lot and listen to the chatter will be a very hard thing to do."

Brian Clough

Q: "Do hooligans deserve a clip round the ear?"

A: "Yes. If some of those had a clip round the ear five years ago, the incident wouldn't have occurred last night."

Chairman Maurice Roworth backs Brian Clough after he smacked pitch invaders

"I am a big-head, not a figurehead."

Brian Clough on why he turned down board positions

"Football attracts a certain percentage of nobodies who want to be somebodies at a football club."

Brian Clough on club directors

"If a chairman sacks the manager he initially appointed, he should go as well."

Brian Clough

"Running a football club gets their photograph on the back pages of newspapers – nowt else would."

Brian Clough on football directors

"They only know where to find the free drink and the free food. If we win, it's, 'Oh Brian, lovely to see you'. If we lose, it's what a b*stard the manager is and lots of muttering behind closed doors."

Brian Clough on board members

THE FUNNIEST FOREST QUOTES... EVER!

CALLING THE SHOTS

"He is due to resume training on Friday. That's fine, but if he looks to be running a bit awkwardly, it will be because I've stuck the olive branch up his bum."

Dave Bassett on Pierre van Hooijdonk's return to the club

"If there was one player I clashed with more than any other during my time in management, it was Martin O'Neill. Management gave him the perfect platform on which he can display his intelligence. He had an opinion on almost anything and was never slow to express it."

Brian Clough on his former midfielder

"When I buy a player, I don't expect to have to teach him to play football."

Brian Clough on Justin Fashanu's technical weaknesses

"There are two reasons why I'm interested in signing you. The first is that there's no one in our club who can play left back and the second is that you're cheap."

Brian Clough to Frank Clark

"The ugliest player I ever signed was Kenny Burns."

Brian Clough

"He's had more holidays than Judith Chalmers."

Brian Clough on Roy Keane's suspensions

"Take your hands out of your pockets."

Brian Clough to Trevor Francis

"When he learns how to trap a ball and kick it, I'll play him."

Brian Clough on Gary Megson

"He's got bigger dimples than Shirley Temple."

Brian Clough on Teddy Sheringham

"He wasn't particularly well-liked by the players anyway."

Dave Bassett on Pierre van Hooijdonk

"I decided to handle [O'Neill] by pretending he was thick. I thought that way I might just shut him up. Of course, it didn't always work, 'cos here was a bloke capable of talking for Ireland. One day he'll be manager of this club [Forest], and I'm going to buy the biggest dictionary I can find, pick out a few words he doesn't know, and when he invites me over for a beer I'm going to drop them into the conversation. I want to see his eyes roll."

Brian Clough on Martin O'Neill

"The problem with him having that great lump on top of his head is that I'm not sure he knows at which angle the ball will come off. It takes him so long to put it up I'm often waiting around to give the team talk."

Frank Clark on Jason Lee's remarkable haircut

"[He was] possibly 10 pounds overweight, indisputably the slowest player in the Football League... He was fat, often unshaven, dressed like a tramp, and smoked one fag after another."

Brian Clough's initial verdict of John Robertson

"I'm wary of people who are more intelligent that I am. But I soon got you down to my level."

Brian Clough to Martin O'Neill

"I don't want troublemakers, I don't want sh*t-houses and I don't want an ugly b*stard like Kenny Burns littering my club."

Brian Clough is reluctant to sign the Scotsman

"I haven't seen the lad but he comes highly recommended by my greengrocer."

Brian Clough on buying Nigel Jemson

"I only hit Roy [Keane] the once. He got up, so I couldn't have hit him that hard."

Brian Clough

"He was fatter than I was. But he used to treat a football better than most people treat a woman."

Brian Clough on John Robertson

Journalist to Trevor Francis: "When will you be making your debut for Nottingham Forest?"

Brian Clough: "When I pick him."

Forest's record-breaking signing is unveiled at a press conference

Brian Clough: "I see you're in the England squad, do you think you're good enough?"

Stuart Pearce: "I'm not sure."

Clough: "I don't, get out!"

The Forest skipper's conversation after his first England call-up

"The idiot on the right side... Clever b*llocks."

Brian Clough describes Martin O'Neill

"You can't head the ball, you can't tackle and you can't chase back."

Brian Clough to Gary McAllister while in talks to sign him from Leicester

"It was a wonderful bit of individual skill and, if you saw it in La Liga this weekend, people would be waxing lyrical about it for weeks. Unfortunately because we have an ugly, ginger-haired centre forward, we probably won't."

Colin Calderwood on Joe Garner's 35-yard goal against Southampton

"Neil Webb won't refuse a contract. He knows that if he turns me down I'll give him our equivalent of the Chinese water torture. I'll lock him in a room with our directors."

Brian Clough

"If I had been the multi-millionaire owner of the club, I would have left him to rot in Holland."

Dave Bassett on Pierre van Hooijdonk

"He's not joining Pisa for the simple and most important reason that his mother decided that days ago."

Brian Clough on reports son Nigel was heading to Serie A

"If I ever felt off-colour I'd sit next to John Robertson. Compared with this fat, dumpy lad, I was Errol Flynn."

Brian Clough

Brian Clough: "Have you found yourself a house yet Dave?"

Dave Currie: "No, not yet boss."

Clough: "Don't bother, son."

A dressing room exchange shortly after the striker arrived from Barnsley. He only lasted eight games at the club

"He didn't look anything like a professional athlete when I first clapped eyes on him. In fact, there were times when he barely resembled a member of the human race."

Brian Clough on John Robertson

"I wish Gary McAllister would stop talking about me. I can only assume I upset him when we met because he was wearing cowboy boots and I asked if he was related to John Wayne."
Brian Clough after the midfielder rejected Forest to join Leeds

Brian Clough: "What the hell are you doing here, son?"
Tommy Gaynor: "You took me off."
Brian Clough: "Oh, I thought you were Phil Starbuck!'"
A chat in the dugout five minutes after a bemused Gaynor was substituted

"He's not actually a very good player but he's got a lovely smile that brightens up my Monday mornings."

Brian Clough on Neil Webb

Martin O'Neill: "Why am I playing for the second team?"

Brian Clough: "Because you're too good for the thirds."

"I wanted two hard b*stards at the centre of that defence."

Brian Clough on Larry Lloyd and Kenny Burns

"He turned up to sign for us in a car without tax or insurance. It's a wonder we weren't arrested."

Brian Clough on Kenny Burns

"He wouldn't have shifted a copy without my mug on the front, my name alongside it and my thoughts on every page."

Brian Clough on Peter Taylor writing a book: 'With Clough, by Taylor'

"The half-time Oxo was better."

Brian Clough on the first time he saw Garry Birtles play in non-league

"Martin O'Neill was like James Joyce. He used words I'd never heard of."

Brian Clough

"Get out of my sight. If I ever see you again, I'll kill you."

Brian Clough to Justin Fashanu after he pulled out of a game with an injury 45 minutes before kick-off

"I could point to Robbo and say, 'You were a tramp when I came here, and now you're the best winger in the game'."

Brian Clough on John Robertson

"My son Nigel, the one who plays centre forward for me at Nottingham Forest, asked me recently if I had any regrets. It was when Peter Taylor had died. I told my son, 'He should have seen you play at Wembley the last couple of times'."

Brian Clough

"Have you ever been hit in the stomach?"

Brian Clough before he hit Nigel Jemson in the stomach

"I looked upon [Martin] O'Neill as a bit of a smart a*se."

Brian Clough

"I'm not saying Brian Rice is thin and pale, but the maid in our hotel made his bed the other day and didn't realise he was still in it."
Brian Clough

"We were arrogant at the bottom and we are arrogant at the top – that's consistency."
Brian Clough on his relationship with Peter Taylor

"What is the point of giving you the ball when there is a genius on the other wing?"
Brian Clough to Martin O'Neill, referring to John Robertson

"Archie Gemmill was five-foot nowt but he could out-jump six-foot opponents. He used to scare Peter Osgood to death."

Brian Clough

"When you learn to play with it, you can have the match ball."

Brian Clough to Peter Withe after he scored four goals against Ipswich

"I'm calling you Edward because that's what it says on your birth certificate."

Brian Clough on meeting Teddy Sheringham

THE FUNNIEST FOREST QUOTES... EVER!

OFF THE PITCH

"One of my sons is studying German – in case they try another invasion!"

Brian Clough

"My wife told me that if I score a hat-trick this year I get a dog, so I was trying to get the penalty."

Eric Lichaj had extra motivation for his treble after scoring a brace in Forest's 4-2 win over Arsenal

"There are more hooligans in the House of Commons than at a football match."

Brian Clough

"Barbara says to me repeatedly, 'I don't care what you do at the ground. When you come into the house, try and smile'."

Brian Clough

"I once told him I'd never be caught standing at a bar having a drink with him. He said the feeling was mutual."

Larry Lloyd on Brian Clough

"Women run everything. The only thing I've done within my house in the past 20 years is recognise Angola as an independent state."

Brian Clough

"When I was admitted to the heart unit, somebody sent me a get-well telegram that said, 'We didn't even know you had one'."
Brian Clough

"My wife said to me in bed, 'God, your feet are cold'. I said, 'You can call me Brian in bed, dear'."
Brian Clough on married life

"I'm convinced that some people in London still think anyone north of the M25 lives in a cave, wears a flat cap and goes whippet racing."
Brian Clough

"I know I had a reputation for being a bit of a boozer... I can remember occasions in Uriah Heep's wine bar in Nottingham when people were staring at me to see what I was going to down. There were times when I would order a glass of milk just to throw them because you couldn't really disguise what I was going to down!"

John Robertson

"He's already taken over my office and the team talk. Now I've taught him to stop eating the carpet at home, he'll learn how to pick the team."

Brian Clough on his dog Del Boy

THE FUNNIEST FOREST QUOTES... EVER!

"Berlin has everything. It is a cosmopolitan city with theatres and the people are open-minded. They are not as narrow-minded like the people in Nottingham. There are no theatres, no cinemas, hardly anything. All Nottingham has is Robin Hood... and he's dead."

Bryan Roy on joining Hertha Berlin

"If I'd been an MP, I'd have wanted to be Speaker. No one else was having the last word."

Brian Clough

"Sinatra met me, you know."

Brian Clough

84

"When he played for me at Nottingham Forest, he was the slowest player in the squad – perhaps due to all those nightclubs he kept telling me he didn't frequent."

Brian Clough after Teddy Sheringham won the 2001 Footballer of the Year award

Q: "What's your favourite drink?"

A: "Alcohol."

Brian Clough in 1983

"I'm ill-tempered, rude and wondering what's for tea, same as ever."

Brian Clough on how it feels being retired

THE FUNNIEST FOREST QUOTES... EVER!

FIELD OF DREAMS

"When I played for Forest at Derby, they were chucking coins and spitting at me when I took throw-ins. And that was just the old ladies."
Stuart Pearce

"We were doing f*ck all in training. People say we became champions, but so what? If you were to change all the managers in the league for cats, at the end of the season there will still be one champion and three will get relegated. Does that mean the cat who is champion is fantastic and the three who got relegated are sh*t?
Pierre van Hooijdonk on Dave Bassett's managerial style

"Would also like to sincerely say thank you to absolutely none of my teammates, as this is an individual award."

Joe Lolley jokes after winning the club's Player of the Year prize

"We won two European Cups and we never practised a free-kick."

Martin O'Neill

"Even then he was off his head, completely crackers. He would put sweets down his socks and then give them to teachers to eat."

Steve Stone on his old school mate Paul Gascoigne

"Which is actually the big club here? Forest can point to two European Cups. How many have Newcastle got? I think we all know the answer to that question!"

Dexter Blackstock after a Newcastle player apparently said Forest would celebrate a win as if they had won the European Cup

"I have never been the DJ because my music is so good that I can turn a changing room into a nightclub and it is not good for our professionalism!"

Guy Moussi

"I once got a 'Red Tree' for asking to go to the toilet on the training ground. I said I needed to go – and was told in no uncertain terms that I should have gone before."
John Robertson on the players' fine that was inserted into a club envelope

Forest website: "It's almost seven months since we were last beaten away from home. What do you put that down to?"
Luke Chambers: "The fact that we didn't play for three months during the summer was a massive help."

"Newcastle and Ruud Gullit came in with a £7m bid, twice what Forest had paid. But [Dave] Bassett told the papers my price was £10m. Ten million! In 1998, that's like putting a price tag on a bottle of water and asking for £25."

Pierre van Hooijdonk

"If I played for Scotland my grandma would be the proudest woman in the country, if she wasn't dead."

Mark Crossley

"I can see the carrot at the end of the tunnel."

Stuart Pearce on his comeback from injury

"We made Coventry look like Brazil, we were that bad."

Dave Beasant after a 4-0 defeat at Highfield Road

"Clough had nicked the washing machine from the laundry room, which [the ladies] weren't too happy about. So that was my signing-on fee – and it wasn't even brand new!"

Larry Lloyd

"I've tried that second free-kick a hundred times and it always ends up in the Trent!"

Ian Woan after his goals against Tottenham in a 1995/96 FA Cup tie

Q: "Any reasons for your current squad number?"

A: "It was what I was given at the start of the season."

Q: "Who is your room mate? Has he any bad habits?"

A: "Brendan Maloney. He doesn't have any bad habits."

Q: "Who do you listen to on the radio?"

A: "I don't listen to the radio too much."

Q: "What other sports are you good at?"

A: "I haven't really got into table tennis like the rest of the lads have since a table was installed at the club last year. It's not really my thing."

Q: "Do you download any podcasts?"

A: "No."

Mark Byrne in the match-day programme

"I remember trying to light this thing in the bloody room to keep insects away but I think Robbo got bitten all over his a*se. Right enough, it was some size of an a*se."

Kenny Burns rooming with Scotland teammate John Robertson at the 1978 World Cup

"I like Nottingham. It's a bit like Ireland. My heart is with this club. My present contract has another three years to go, and I did have another one of three years in mind, but now I fancy something a bit longer."

Roy Keane, six months before leaving for Manchester United

"The defeat to Accrington was harder than that."

Grant Holt mocks Charlton after dumping them out of the FA Cup

"I thought we were going to look at some peas – as in, garden peas. I mean, peas are peas, aren't they? Green things. What kind of peas are sweet peas? I know what green peas are. I know mushy peas. In Scotland, flowers are just things whose heads you kick off when you've had a few pints on a Saturday night."

Kenny Burns on meeting Brian Clough at a garden centre exhibiting sweet peas

Field Of Dreams

"It was funny running up the wing and having my brother alongside me on the touchline. He could have booked me because I kept taking the mickey out of him. 'Oi, you ginger d*ck head' is one thing I remember calling him."
Stuart Pearce on his brother Ray who was a linesman at Forest's game with Brighton

"[Clough] took me off in Toronto on a tour where the referee asked me to pull my socks up for the national anthem, and I told him where to go. We were all lined up for the kick-off and up went No.5 and he dragged me off before a ball was bloody kicked!"
Larry Lloyd

THE FUNNIEST FOREST QUOTES... EVER!

CALL THE MANAGER

"I jump into a dugout and I'm waiting thinking, 'Come on let's get started' as we are playing Arsenal. I just happened to look around and I'm stood with Dennis Bergkamp, Patrick Vieira, Nelson Vivas and I thought, 'How are we bottom of the league with these in the team?' I was obviously in the wrong dugout and they show it on television even now."

Ron Atkinson's hilarious dugout mistake

"No disrespect to Dave Bassett... but I've just been relegated 'cos we've been p*ssed on by a team who can't particularly play."

Brian Clough after defeat to Sheffield United sent Forest down

"The difference, in a nutshell, was that they had two very good strikers, who got them goals, and an excellent keeper who kept them in the match."

Dougie Freedman in 'better players win matches' shock

"If I catch spectators on my pitch in future, I know exactly what I'll do. They'll get another clip around the earhole. I hit five pitch invaders – and I would have got all 300 if I could."

Brian Clough on hitting fans who came onto the field against QPR

"There, that's better."

Brian Clough spits on Darren Wassall's injured hand after the defender requested to be substituted in a reserve game

"You have to win your home games at home."

Colin Calderwood after Forest drew with Doncaster

"You get the feeling you are supposed to go to Old Trafford and let them walk all over you."

Frank Clark after Alex Ferguson criticised Forest for time-wasting and fouling in their 2-1 victory

"Our Elizabeth could have put it in."

Brian Clough on Trevor Francis' winner in the 1979 European Cup Final

"Tell him he's Pele and that he's playing up front for the last 10 minutes."

Brian Clough after Stuart Pearce suffered concussion

"It wasn't a great game but they were a boring team, Malmo. In fact the Swedes are quite a boring nation. But we still won, so who cares?"

Brian Clough after the famous European victory

"Asa Hartford kept dashing off to mark Mick Mills when we played Ipswich. I got a message out to him saying if he wanted to meet Mills that badly I could arrange an interview after the game."

Brian Clough

"We've hit rock bottom – we're having the sh*t kicked out of us."

Assistant manager Micky Adams after Forest were knocked out of the FA Cup by Portsmouth

"I think I will go home and slash my wrists."

Joe Kinnear after a 4-1 loss to Coventry

"He was out of order kneeing me in the back of the leg. I don't mind him doing it to my face, but to do it behind my back was a bit cowardly."
Billy Davies is angry with Derby manager Nigel Clough

"He pleased his mum."
Brian Clough after son Nigel's goal against Luton in the 1988 League Cup Final

"If we'd kept a clean sheet tonight we'd have won 1-0."
Steve Cotterill on a 2-1 defeat against Middlesbrough

THE FUNNIEST FOREST QUOTES... EVER!

Printed in Great Britain
by Amazon

49448018R00059